Beatrix Potter

BOOK CLUB ORGANIZER

Gift children with a rich and memorable learning experience! Plan a Beatrix Potter book club with this step-by-step planner and organizer, to use at home or with friends.

Hosanna Rodriguez

ALSO BY HOSANNA RODRIGUEZ

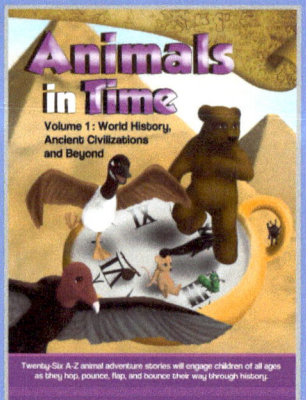 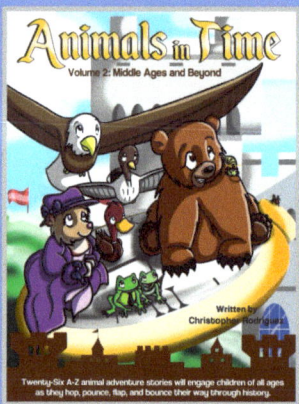 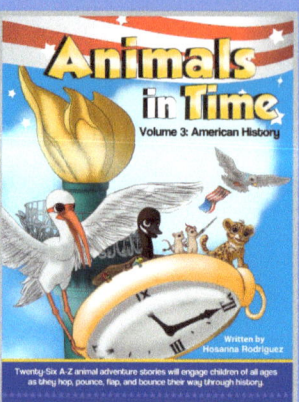

Animals in Time: History told through the eyes of animals.

WWW.LETSLEARNKIDS.COM

Beatrix Potter Book Club Organizer Copyright © 2016 by Hosanna Rodriguez. All rights reserved.

Letslearnkids.hosanna@gmail.com

Cover design by Genesis Moss
Front cover photograph by Jennifer Chou at Pingo Lingo Photography
Proofread by Traci Post

All hand-sketched images by Jaden Rodriguez (age 9)

Special thanks to Walter, my Incredible Hulk of a husband who helps and encourages me through life's many adventures, including technical and moral support to finish a project like this book club organizer. And to our own set of flopsy bunnies—Christopher, Jaden, Juliana, and Christina—my all-time favorite reading pals! Many thanks also to Lorraine, Cassidy, Tina, Carrie, and Jamie for working with me through the kinks of our weekly book clubs, and for being the amazing, supportive, and fun-loving friends that they are! And I can't forget Harrison and Carmen for design consultation!

For beautiful and customized book club products, visit us at:

WWW.LETSLEARNKIDS.COM

ISBN 978-0-9963258-1-3

TO MY SWEET BUNNIES.

AND TO ALL THE OTHER
BUNNY PALS OUT THERE!

Sweet stories and a vivid imagination make for a magical childhood…

"There is something delicious about writing the first words of a story. You never quite know where they'll take you."

"I remember I used to half believe and wholly play with fairies when I was a child. What heaven can be more real than to retain the spirit-world of childhood, tempered and balanced by knowledge and common-sense."

~Beatrix Potter

Beatrix Potter Book Club

*Photo by Lorraine Lewis

Contents

The Tale of Peter Rabbit...................1

The Tale of Benjamin Bunny.....7

The Tale of Mrs. Tiggy-Winkle........15

The Tale of Jemima Puddle-Duck........23

The Tale of the Flopsy Bunnies...31

The Tale of Tom Kitten..................39

The Tale of Mr. Jeremy Fisher....47

The Tale of Mrs. Tittlemouse party...55

Pre-Planning......71

Shopping Lists....77

Templates..........81

Introduction

Stories make me laugh.
Stories make me dream.
They can make my heart race and my eyes tear.
Stories are meant to be shared, and whom
better to savor them with than children . . .
the masters of imagination!

A FEW THOUGHTS FROM HOSANNA . . .

There are those special stories that are too irresistibly wonderful to keep to myself . . . so, I share them with children. It's impossible to begin to count the magical moments spent cuddling with my children, giggling, eager to turn the page to see what happens next. Often we would pause to reflect together on the peril that befell a main character. Other times we would remark on how wonderful it would be to eat the foods so deliciously described or make a game out of an adventure so intriguingly portrayed in the pages of the book.

A book club has the potential to unite people of all ages in their shared interest of experiencing something special through the power of well-crafted stories, in building relationships, in sharing thoughts and creative expression from a personal interpretation of what has been read, in developing various skills, and in having a whole lot of fun! It is out of the desire to encourage adults to not only enjoy the world of stories with children, but to also bring *others* together in this pursuit, that this Beatrix Potter Book Club Organizer was created. This guide provides a parent, family member, teacher, and anyone else who's looking, with ways to intentionally encourage the children in their life to develop a love for literature while building relationships.

In the years to come, may wide smiles and beautiful memories fill you each time you remember your Beatrix Potter Book Club days.

Lots of Love,

Hosanna

A Purpose And A Plan

THERE'S A LOT MORE TO A BOOK CLUB THAN MEETS THE EYE!

A good story stands on its own and does not require anything more to improve its timeless qualities. There are ways, however, to develop a rich and relevant method of learning by integrating the story with the basic skills every child needs to learn, by wrapping them up in the characters and plot of a winning tale. We can make the most of learning in a book club!

SKILLS

Diane Lockman, founder of Classical Scholar, is an expert at defining skills and teaching how to incorporate them into school plans and everyday activities. She categorizes them into three main topics: Reading, Critical Thinking, and Writing/Public Speaking.

Ms. Lockman advocates starting with the basics with these foundational skills and says, "Simple concepts precede complex concepts."

And that is exactly what we are doing for our young ones here—starting with simple concepts that will lay a foundation for more complex concepts in their futures.

(Visit her website for an in-depth look at the skills: www.classicalscholar.com.)

Reading (language skills)
Reading the rich language of the Beatrix stories takes skill, and this book club includes several activities to help strengthen these skills. One key element is the **notebook**, where children record thoughts about the stories through words, sketches, etc. (written by child or dictated to parent if child is not writing yet).

Critical Thinking (analytical skills)
These skills include listening carefully (following story, circle time, steps to activities), solving problems (how to build a bird's nest, where to dig bunny tunnels), and observation (planting seeds and watching them grow). These are just a few of the ways we bolster critical thinking skills in our book club.

Writing & Public Speaking (communication skills)
Our little ones' futures will be brighter if they learn to communicate ideas clearly. Circle time is a good time to discuss the stories and animals, but they will also present a Beatrix Potter poem or portion of a story the final day.

MULTISENSORY LEARNING

Children learn in a multisensory approach, using two or more senses to take in information about their world in a variety of ways. This book club is packed full of multisensory learning activities, from start to finish, involving tasting, digging, building, smelling, listening, and on and on. They will strengthen fine and gross motor skills each day with this one-of-a-kind active learning opportunity. No passive learning in this type of book club!

RELATIONSHIP BUILDING

Connecting with others and learning how to work as a team are vital elements for successful relationships within families, communities, and workplaces. Friendships cannot be forced, but nurturing and cultivating relationships are necessary for healthy interaction. Kids need it, and parents need it; so we all benefit from the fun times to be had in book clubs.

HOW TO USE THIS ORGANIZER . . .

Step 1: Gather a group of friends to join you in a Beatrix Potter book club.

Step 2: Encourage each adult to get a copy of the Beatrix Potter Book Club Organizer and Beatrix Potter original, unabridged stories.

Step 3: Plan Who, What, and Where. Schedule a get-together with the adults to plan the details (when and where to meet, who will cover each activity and snack, who will shop for materials and what will be the price range of those materials, and what will be the overall goals for your club). Tip: We began ours in early April in order to finish by May. Not only is spring a charming time to hold a Beatrix Potter book club, but our children also had a gift prepared in time for Mother's Day (a lavender sachet and handmade card).

Step 4: Prep Time! Once materials have been purchased, plan a prep day, or night, to have as much as possible ready for little hands to begin working. (See pre-planning steps in pages 71-76.)

Step 5: Plan, but stay flexible. If you have any experience with working with children, you will know that even the best laid plans take a different shape than first imagined, at least to some extent, and flexibility is a *must*. I have provided you with detailed instructions for all activities and have shared steps for planning details ahead of time for an organized approach to a promising book club, along with shopping lists, templates, places to keep notes and member contact information; but let me assure you, even with all this help, expect some amount of chaos to occur from time to time. Such is the nature with children, so embrace it and don't be afraid to adjust your plans based on the needs of those involved.

Step 6: Customize your approach. Use this organizer as a springboard for a customized book club experience you envision will suit the needs and interests of your group. Look at each activity provided here and decide which direction to take it. For example, you may want to simplify an activity such as modifying the activity of sewing bunny ears by using basic paper and glue, OR you may choose to elaborate on my rudimentary efforts at sewing (I am not an expert seamstress by any means) and develop a more elaborate version for your children to follow. There is space for your notes within the pages of the book club outline as well as at the end of each section. Jot down your ideas in whatever way works best for you. Adjust each activity to suit your goals.

Step 7: Tips to help your book club run smoothly.
- **Specify adult involvement.** Unless you have an adult who would like to carry the bulk of the book club on his or her shoulders solo (which is doubtful and unrealistic), delegating responsibilities is crucial. In order to maximize the potential learning experience by utilizing the individual talents of each adult AND to minimize the risk of burnout for any particular person, commit to *learn how to work together*. Areas of responsibilities can be split into stations. Here are a few possible "station" ideas:
    1. Who will bring supplies each week?
    2. Who will bring snacks? (Rotating snacks works well.)
    3. Who will lead circle time?
    4. Who will lead each activity?
- **Read stories at home before meeting.**
- **Bring a visual aid to circle time that pertains to the animal of the week, such as a library book, picture, puppet, etc.**

Book Club Pals

Parent's Name(s)_____

Child's Name_____

Phone #_____

Email Address_____

Other Info_____

_____

Parent's Name(s)_____

Child's Name_____

Phone #_____

Email Address_____

Other Info_____

_____

Parent's Name(s)_____

Child's Name_____

Phone #_____

Email Address_____

Other Info_____

_____

Parent's Name(s)_____

Child's Name_____

Phone #_____

Email Address_____

Other Info_____

_____

Parent's Name(s)_____

Child's Name_____

Phone #_____

Email Address_____

Other Info_____

_____

Parent's Name(s)_____

Child's Name_____

Phone #_____

Email Address_____

Other Info_____

_____

Parent's Name(s)_____

Child's Name_____

Phone #_____

Email Address_____

Other Info_____

_____

Parent's Name(s)_____

Child's Name_____

Phone #_____

Email Address_____

Other Info_____

_____

Peter Rabbit

Once upon a time there were four little Rabbits, and their names were—

Flopsy,

Mopsy,

Cotton-tail,

and Peter.

They lived with their Mother in a sand-bank, underneath the root of a very big fir-tree.

~Beatrix Potter

The Tale Of Peter Rabbit

NOTES
Location & Time:
_____

Fun for the day:
- Circle time
- Snack
- Paint pails
- Make bunny ears
- Decorate bunny books and bookmarks
- Flower pounding

Snack:
milk
blackberries
bread with currants
(raisin bread)

Circle Time Discussion Suggestions:
* children (and adults) introduce themselves, including pets... *fitting since these stories revolve around animals!*
* characters in the story, including rabbit siblings and other animals briefly mentioned—cat, birds, fish, mouse
* favorite or suspenseful parts of story
* **introduce concept behind notebooks they will make**

Fun Facts About Rabbits:
* rabbits are born blind
* a baby rabbit is called a kit (or kitten)
* rabbits are herbivores, eating mostly grasses and other plants
* a rabbit's teeth never stop growing

Painting Pails

The first activity we started with after circle time was painting the pails in order to give them time to dry (which was a relatively quick process).

NOTES

Materials:
- pre-scrubbed pails
- stencils (or sponge shapes for design)
- acrylic paints
- foam brushes (or sponges)
- clear acrylic sealer
- paper plates for children's selection of paint colors
- paper towels (or rags)

Steps:
1. Paint base color (if child desires a base color).
2. Add design (using stencils, sponges, markers).
3. Add child's name somewhere on the pail.
4. Spray entire surface with acrylic sealer.

THE TALE OF PETER RABBIT ✳ 2

Bunny Ears

Materials:
- ☐ prepared ears
- ☐ thread
- ☐ long needles
- ☐ cotton balls
- ☐ bells
- ☐ Velcro

 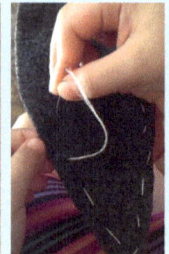 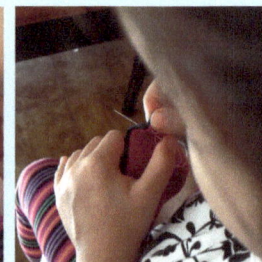 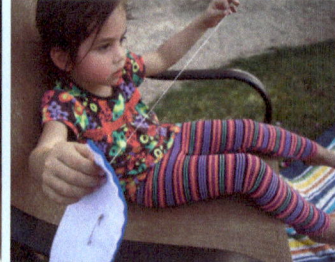  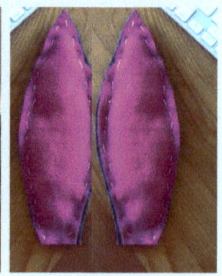

Steps:
1. Match 2 felt ear pieces together (1 with stick & 1 without) and, starting at a lower corner, stitch three-quarters of the way around ear, leaving opening to add cotton and bell.
2. After stretching cotton balls, insert cotton and bell; finish stitching. Repeat for second ear.

   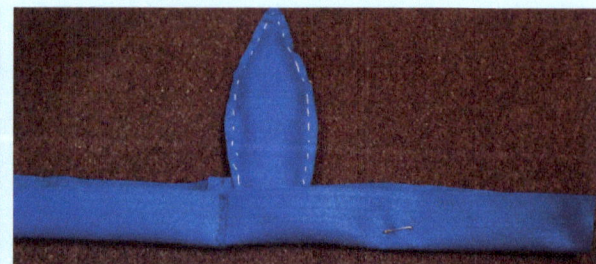

3. After 2 ears have been sewn, sew headband strips together on one end. *Measure headband width & distance between ears.
4. Fold over almost halfway (lengthwise), and restitch sewn ends together.
5. Slip 1 ear in opening and sew from that end of headband to just beyond that ear. Place second ear in headband opening and continue sewing all the way to the end of headband.
6. Attach Velcro strip to either end of the headband. (I secured with hot glue.)
7. Adorn with flower, large button, etc.

NOTES

Flower Pounding

Bunny Books

Bookmarks

Materials:
- prepared books and bookmarks
- round river stones or wooden mallets
- waxed paper
- clear acrylic sealer (optional)
- fresh flowers or leaves

Steps:
1. Gather fresh flowers and/or leaves.
2. Write child's name on notebook cover.
3. Arrange plants on the bookmark and notebook cover.
4. Lay a sheet of waxed paper on top of plants.
5. Gently pound the waxed paper with plants beneath it with rock or mallet.
6. Spray with acrylic sealer and allow to dry.

THE TALE OF PETER RABBIT ✱ 4

Peter Rabbit

LOCATION:

DATE/TIME:

SNACK:

ACTIVITY 1:
- **LEADER:**
- **NOTES:**

ACTIVITY 2:
- **LEADER:**
- **NOTES:**

ACTIVITY 3:
- **LEADER:**
- **NOTES:**

ACTIVITY 4:
- **LEADER:**
- **NOTES:**

NOTES

Benjamin Bunny

One morning a little rabbit sat on a bank.
He pricked his ears and listened to the trit-trot,
trit-trot of a pony.

~Beatrix Potter

The Tale Of Benjamin Bunny

Fun for the day:
- Circle time
- Snack
- Paint pots
- Bunny tunnels
- Bunny hopping races

NOTES
Location & Time:
_____

Circle Time Discussion Suggestions:
* characters in the story, including Benjamin's cousins, Old Mr. Benjamin Bunny, Old Mrs. Rabbit (Peter's mother), Mr. McGregor, and other animals (cat, birds, mice)
* favorite or suspenseful parts of story
* invite them to try winking, as the mice cracking cherry-stones winked at Peter and Benjamin
* **invite children to share their notebooks**

Snack: rosemary tea (chamomile w/rosemary) pears crackers

Fun Facts About Rabbit Homes:
* most live in tunnels (burrows) called warrens
* the tunnels are almost always dug and created by females
* rabbit warrens locations can range from prairies to forests to desserts to beaches

Painted Pots

Materials:
- pots and trays
- patio paint or standard acrylic paint
- sponges or brushes (we used foam brushes)
- clear acrylic sealer (if using standard acrylic)
- stencils (optional)
- tall, narrow cylinders (oatmeal or Pringles canisters)
- paper plates
- newspaper
- box or tote to hold all pots and trays once finished

NOTES

*If you don't have time to apply acrylic sealer, make sure to do so within the next 4 weeks, before Jeremy Fisher meeting, when seeds are planted.

Steps:
1. Paint inside of pot.
2. Turn pot upside down and place on canister base.
3. Paint entire surface of pot, including the bottom and top rim of the pot. *Apply a second coat of paint if first coat didn't cover pot well enough. You may need to wait 20 minutes or so to allow it to dry between coats.*
4. Once paint has dried, paint design on pot using flexible stencils, sponge cut in a desired shape, or freehand design with brush.
5. If using standard acrylic sealer, apply acrylic sealer and allow to dry.
6. Recommendation: one parent should keep all pots and trays until Jemima Puddle-Duck gathering.

THE TALE OF BENJAMIN BUNNY ✲ 10

Bunny Tunnels

"That wood was full of rabbit holes; and in the neatest sandiest hole of all, lived Benjamin's aunt and his cousins—Flopsy, Mopsy, Cotton-tail and Peter." ~ B.P.

We placed our bunny in the watering can, on one side of the plot of mud, and the makeshift Mr. McGregor's scarecrow on the other. Objective: help the bunny retrieve its clothing located on the scarecrow, digging tunnels from bunny to scarecrow.

NOTES

Materials:
- ☐ mud
- ☐ digging tools: (trowels, shovels, spoons)

Steps:
1. Allow kids time to play freely in the mud with digging tools.
2. After free time in the mud, encourage them to dig rabbit tunnels, establishing a start and stop marker.

Bunny Hopping Races

The variety of movements encouraged during hopping races will help children develop gross motor skills, balance, coordination, and speed; and they'll have loads of fun at the same time!

Steps:
1. With start and finish lines established, a parent (or older sibling), should demonstrate the move before the race begins.
2. Possible race options:
    - standard run
    - standard skip
    - one-legged hop
    - two-legged hop
    - sideways shuffle

NOTES

THE TALE OF BENJAMIN BUNNY ✻ 12

BENJAMIN BUNNY

LOCATION:	
DATE/TIME:	
SNACK:	

ACTIVITY 1:	
LEADER:	
NOTES:	

ACTIVITY 2:	
LEADER:	
NOTES:	

ACTIVITY 3:	
LEADER:	
NOTES:	

ACTIVITY 4:	
LEADER:	
NOTES:	

NOTES

Mrs. Tiggy-Winkle

Once upon a time there was a little girl called Lucie, who lived at a farm called Little-town. She was a good little girl—only she was always losing her pocket-handkerchiefs!

~Beatrix Potter

THE TALE OF MRS. TIGGY-WINKLE

NOTES
Location & Time:
_____

Fun for the day:
- Circle time
- Snack
- Decorate sachets
- Follow handkerchief trail game
- Sally Henny-Penny kicking game
- Washing laundry and hanging to dry on clothesline

Circle Time Discussion Suggestions:
* characters in the story, including Lucie, Tabby Kitten, Sally Henny-Penny (a speckled hen), Cock Robin, Jenny Wren, old Mrs. Rabbit, Tom Tittlemouse, little lambs, Squirrel Nutkin, Peter Rabbit, Benjamin Bunny
* favorite parts of story
* **invite children to share their notebooks**

Snack: crackers, grape juice (spilled currant wine on tablecloth)

Fun Facts About Hedgehogs:
* baby hedgehogs are called hoglets
* the spikes on their backs are called quills; adults have long, sharp quills, and hoglets have short, soft ones
* they sleep during the day (nocturnal)
* they dig for food with their snouts and claws
* they eat insects, worms, snails, frogs, and sometimes snakes

Decorating Sachets

Fabric markers are an alternative to paint.

See week of Tale of Tom Kitten for using stamps.

Materials:
- pre-cut dish towels
- patio paint or standard acrylic paint
- sponges or brushes (we used foam brushes)
- stencils or stamps (optional)
- paper plates
- newspaper
- zipper sandwich bags

Steps:
1. Children will choose colors and design.
2. They will then apply the paint to the fabric. *Adult may need to hold the fabric in place. Also, less paint is better with the sachet, otherwise the fabric becomes stiff if the entire surface is covered with paint. Sachets will be filled in a later activity.

Handkerchief Trail Game

Materials:
- large basket
- small clothing (child's or doll's)
- handkerchiefs (optional)
- painted pails

Steps:
1. All children will gather in one location.
2. One child (or set of siblings), along with parent (or adult), will be chosen to carry the basket full of laundry.
3. While the rest of the children count to a designated number (possibly 30 or 60 seconds) with eyes closed, the chosen child and parent will leave a trail of clothing and return when time is up.
4. The children who counted will then follow the trail as a group, collecting items in their pails along the way.
5. Then another child, and parent, will leave a trail of laundry as the group counts, until all children have had a chance.

THE TALE OF MRS. TIGGY-WINKLE

Sally Henny-Penny Kicking Game

"And what are those long yellow things with fingers like gloves?" asked Lucie.

Sally Henny-Penny was a speckled hen who was seen constantly scratching and kicking at the ground. Mrs. Tiggy-Winkle cared for the hen's stockings.

In this game, our little chickies kicked a small balloon as if it were a corn kernel, or some other small object. My only regret was that I did not manage to get yellow gloves!

*A word of caution: have a spare balloon, or ball, on hand in case any little munchkin charges ahead and stomps on the balloon before you can say otherwise. I write from experience. Ha!

Materials:
☐ yellow dish gloves (1 set per child)
☐ 2 small balloons, or balls

Steps:
1. Help children put gloves on their feet.
2. Let them scratch at the ground and kick the balloon.

NOTES

Washing Day

Washing day was a big hit with the kids! They could have continued scrubbing, wringing, and hanging all day. This is a fun hand-strengthening project involving team work.

Materials:
- washing basin or bucket
- liquid soap
- washboard (optional)
- clothespins
- thin rope for parents to create a clothesline
- water
- plastic bag to carry wet clothes

Steps:
1. Have a child pour a little soap in basin.
2. Add water.
3. Add clothes, and scrub away!
4. Show children how to wring water from laundry.
5. Show them how to hang and clip laundry to the lines.

Mrs. Tiggy-Winkle

LOCATION:	
DATE/TIME:	
SNACK:	

ACTIVITY 1:	
LEADER:	
NOTES:	

ACTIVITY 2:	
LEADER:	
NOTES:	

ACTIVITY 3:	
LEADER:	
NOTES:	

ACTIVITY 4:	
LEADER:	
NOTES:	

NOTES

Jemima Puddle-Duck

What a funny sight it is to see a brood of ducklings with a hen!

—Listen to the story of Jemima Puddle-Duck, who was annoyed because the farmer's wife would not let her hatch her own eggs.

~Beatrix Potter

The Tale Of Jemima Puddle-Duck

NOTES
Location & Time:
_____

Fun for the day:
- Circle time
- Natural egg dying
- Make giant duck's nest
- Snack
- Plant seeds in egg shells
- *Optional activity: egg roll race with long-handled spoon*

Circle Time Discussion Suggestions:
* characters in the story, including farmer's wife, Rebeccah Puddle-Duck, foxy-whiskered gentleman, collie-dog Kep, two foxhound puppies
* what are shawls and bonnets
* what materials ducks, and birds in general, use to make nests
* favorite parts, and suspenseful parts, of story. (My daughter was enthralled by the hero of the story, collie-dog Kep, so I read to all the children the section of the story from when Jemima was describing the fox until, "And nothing more was ever seen of that foxy-whiskered gentleman." I also invited them to bark, bay, growl, howl, squeal, and groan as I read about the confrontation between puppies, collie-dog, and fox.)
* **invite children to share their notebooks**

Snack: boiled eggs, oatmeal cookies (oats fox promised to feed Jemima)

Fun Facts About Ducks:
* baby ducks are called ducklings, adult males are drakes, and adult females are hens
* they have waterproof feathers
* nests are made out of mother's down feathers, grasses, mud, leaves, and twigs

Natural Egg Dying (1)

What is a story about Jemima Puddle-Duck without eggs? I decided to color our eggs using natural ingredients instead of dyes, and I was surprised by the resulting colors. The one that surprised me the most was the speckled lavender. For some reason, the grape juice and vinegar made small bubbles on the egg, causing an uneven coloring. "Ugh!" was my first reaction. These were not the pretty eggs I had hoped for. I figured they were a lost cause and let the kids rub them with water in a bowl. The result was nearly shocking! With the dark, dirty-looking blue-gray film rubbed off, a gentle speckled pattern emerged. It reminded me of the lesson behind *The Ugly Duckling*.

NOTES

speckled lavender

   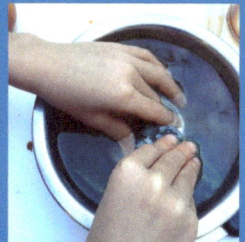 

Materials:
- ☐ 1 cup grape juice
- ☐ 1 TBSP white vinegar
- ☐ white eggs
- ☐ slotted spoon

Steps:
1. Place eggs in pot with room temperature water and bring to boil. Then remove from heat, cover pot, and let eggs sit in hot water for 18 minutes.
2. Remove eggs, and place in ice water until cooled.
3. Mix together juice and vinegar in separate container, and add eggs until desired color. Gently rub egg in water to remove excess film for speckled look.

faint red-orange

    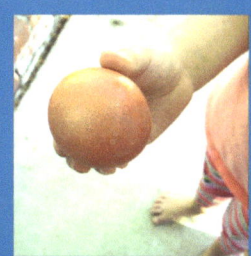

Materials:
- ☐ 2 TBSP paprika
- ☐ 1 cup boiling water
- ☐ 2 tsp white vinegar
- ☐ white eggs
- ☐ slotted spoon

Steps:
1. Follow cooking process from Step 1 and 2, above.
2. In a separate container, mix paprika into 1 cup boiling water, then add vinegar.
3. Add boiled eggs to paprika solution until desired color (at least 30 minutes).

Natural Egg Dying (2)

The kids enjoyed smelling and mixing the juices and spices together!

deep gold

One color I did not manage to document with pictures during coloring process was the deep gold. I simply boiled uncooked, white eggs in 1 quart of water with 3 TBSP of turmeric spice and 2 TBSP of white vinegar for 30 minutes. As you can see in the picture to the left, they were bright and beautiful!

royal blue

Materials:
- 4 cups chopped red cabbage
- 1 quart water
- 2 TBSP white vinegar
- boiled white eggs

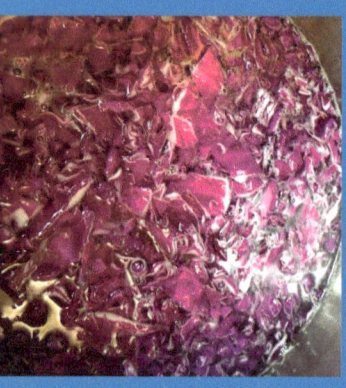

NOTES

Steps:
1. Bring cabbage, water, and vinegar to boil, then lower heat and simmer for 30 mins.
2. Cool cabbage solution to room temperature.
3. Soak boiled eggs in solution for 30 mins, at minimum.

dark, rich brown

Materials:
- 1 quart strong black coffee
- 2 TBSP white vinegar
- uncooked white eggs

Steps:
1. Boil eggs in black coffee for 30 minutes.
2. Cool in ice water.

Make Giant Duck's Nest

Can you spot the sly fox sneaking up on the unassuming brood of ducklings?

As you can see, they had a blast making this giant nest. They gathered materials and then plopped down in the middle of it as ducklings.

Before the ducks were released to gather materials for their nest, the older siblings were put to work scattering the stuffing of a large pillow that was ready to be retired.

Plant Seeds in Eggshells

Materials:
- ☐ eggshells
- ☐ planting soil
- ☐ flower seeds
- ☐ spoons
- ☐ spray bottle for water
- ☐ individual egg carton sections

Steps:
1. Give each child a cut-out section of egg carton to use as a base.
2. Give each child a prepped eggshell to place in their "base."
3. Give each child a spoon, and allow them to scoop soil into the cup, filling half the egg.
4. Have each child sprinkle a pinch of seeds in their shell.
5. Cover seeds with more soil and spray with water.
6. Label each egg or base with name.
7. Assign an adult to keep & water eggs until later planted in pots.

THE TALE OF JEMIMA PUDDLE-DUCK ✻ 28

Jemima Puddle-Duck

LOCATION:	
DATE/TIME:	
SNACK:	

ACTIVITY 1:	
LEADER:	
NOTES:	

ACTIVITY 2:	
LEADER:	
NOTES:	

ACTIVITY 3:	
LEADER:	
NOTES:	

ACTIVITY 4:	
LEADER:	
NOTES:	

NOTES

Flopsy Bunnies

When Benjamin Bunny grew up, he married his Cousin Flopsy. They had a large family, and they were very improvident and cheerful.

I do not remember the separate names of their children; they were generally called the "Flopsy Bunnies."

~Beatrix Potter

The Tale Of The Flopsy-Bunnies

Fun for the day:
- Circle time
- Guess what's in the sack game
- Wash, peel, cut, and steam veggies
- Sack hop race
- Snack time
- Gather items in pails for trash heap
- Fill, scoop, sort, and arrange items in trash heap
- Optional activity: guess the number of squeaker rabbits. All you need are trees, squeaking "bunnies" hiding behind trees, and one bunny (with eyes closed), to guess how many hiding rabbits there are based on squeaks.

"It is said that the effect of eating too much lettuce is 'soporific.' " ~ B.P.

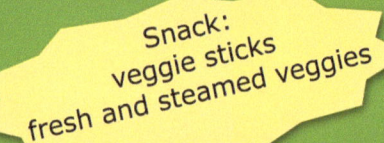

Snack: veggie sticks fresh and steamed veggies

Circle Time Discussion Suggestions:
* characters in the story, including Benjamin Bunny (father), Cousin Flopsy (mother), Peter Rabbit (uncle), Mr. and Mrs. McGregor, Thomasina Tittlemouse
* discuss what has a "soporific" effect on the children and what they do when they feel that way
* items in trash heap (jam pots, paper bags, rotten marrows, grass)
* favorite parts of story
* **invite children to share their notebooks**

Fun Facts About Marrows:
* marrows are summer squash and related to a zucchini
* they can grow as big as a watermelon
* they are yummy steamed or in stews

NOTES

Location & Time:
_____

33 ✻ BEATRIX POTTER BOOK CLUB ORGANIZER

What's in the Sack Game

Notes

Materials:
- pillowcase or large sack
- items that may pertain to Beatrix Potter stories and that have a variety of textures (rolling pin, stuffed animal, pinecone, colander, carrot, etc.)

Steps:
1. Show children the items they will search for in the sack.
2. Place items in sack.
3. Start with a child on one side of the circle, eyes closed, and allow them to feel the item, guessing what it is before they pull it out. Continue with each child.

Prepare Veggie Snack

Materials:
- fresh vegetables (carrots, zucchini, turnips, squash, lettuce, etc.)
- vegetable brush for washing
- peelers, cutting board, knife
- dish towels
- steamer or pot with steamer basket

Steps:
1. Assign children with tasks: washing lettuce, scrubbing veggies, etc.
2. Adult assistance for cutting.
3. Steam squash and any other veggies you want cooked.

*While the squash cooks, the children can enjoy their sack hop race.

THE TALE OF THE FLOPSY BUNNIES ✳ 34

Sack Hop Race

Materials:
- pillowcases
- bunny ears
- long string, rope, or ribbon for finish line

Steps:
1. Help children put on their bunny ears and step into pillowcases.
2. Have adults, or older siblings, hold ends of the rope to secure finish line.
3. Tell your little hopping bunnies how the race will begin. You might sound the call with, "One, two, three *leetle* rabbits…GO!"

*If there is a significant age or height difference between children, you might want to let the little ones have a head start.

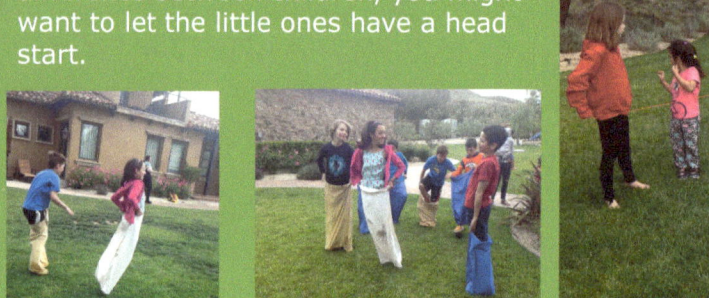

(Even the big kids had to join in on the race!)

NOTES

Snack Time!

Serve steamed and fresh veggies and veggie sticks.

Sometimes kids will try unfamiliar foods in a new setting, especially if role playing is part of the package. Since they are likely to be feeling like bunnies today, they may experiment with turnips and other vegetables that they may have previously refused. Let the healthy eating habits begin!

Make Your Own Trash Heap

"Mr. McGregor's rubbish heap was a mixture. There were jam pots and paper bags, and mountains of chopped grass from the mowing machine (which always tasted oily), and some rotten vegetable marrows..." ~ B.P.

Materials:
- pails for collecting materials
- pots, jars, canisters, scoops, spoons
- natural items collected (pebbles, leaves, grass, sand, etc.)

Steps:
1. Set up pots, jars, and other items.
2. Encourage children to gather materials for their trash heap.
3. Allow them to bring their materials together for filling, scooping, sorting, and arranging.

NOTES

Flopsy Bunnies

LOCATION:	
DATE/TIME:	
SNACK:	
ACTIVITY 1:	
LEADER:	
NOTES:	
ACTIVITY 2:	
LEADER:	
NOTES:	
ACTIVITY 3:	
LEADER:	
NOTES:	
ACTIVITY 4:	
LEADER:	
NOTES:	

NOTES

I wonder who has lost their buttons!

Tom Kitten

Once upon a time there were three little kittens, and their names were Mittens, Tom Kitten, and Moppet.

They had dear little fur coats of their own; and they tumbled about the doorstep and played in the dust.

~Beatrix Potter

The Tale Of Tom Kitten

NOTES

Location & Time:
_____

Fun for the day:
- Circle time
- Snack
- Make scented paint
- Fill sachets with lavender
- Paint cards
- Button Trail Search

Circle Time Discussion Suggestions:

* characters in the story, including Mittens, Moppet, Tabitha Twitchit (mother), Sally Henny Penny, Puddle-Ducks
* favorite parts of story
* purpose of buttons
* if children have ever seen ducks dunking their heads in water (perhaps they are looking for Tom Kitten's clothes)
* **invite children to share their notebooks**

Fun Facts About Cats:

* a male cat is called a tomcat and a female cat is called a queen
* cats greet each other by touching their noses together
* they have rough tongues that they use to clean and groom themselves
* they have 5 toes on each front paw, but only 4 toes on each back paw

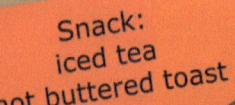

Snack:
iced tea
hot buttered toast

41 * BEATRIX POTTER BOOK CLUB ORGANIZER

Filling Sachets

Between finishing the sachets, making scented paint, and painting the greeting cards; there was a flurry of activity, with many little hands eager to mix, shred, or paint, so we set all the materials on one large table, with multiple stations. A few children who missed our first day of decorating sachets during the week of Mrs. Tiggy-Winkle decorated their sachets with paint and stamps.

Materials (for filling sachets):
- decorated sachets from earlier activity
- dried lavender
- lavender essential oil for longer-lasting fragrance (recommended)
- plastic sandwich bags to hold each filled sachet
- safety pin or sewing pin

Materials (for funnel):
- sheet of paper
- tape

Steps:
1. Make funnel by twisting paper and securing with tape.
2. While one person holds the sachet with its open end up, another holds funnel and pours lavender into the sachet.
3. Pin the opening in sachet closed, and place sachet in plastic sandwich bag to store until opening is sewn shut.

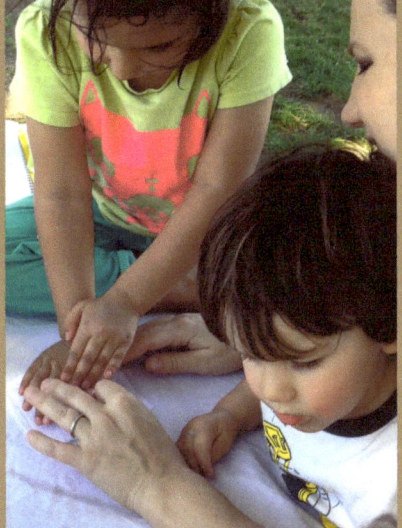

   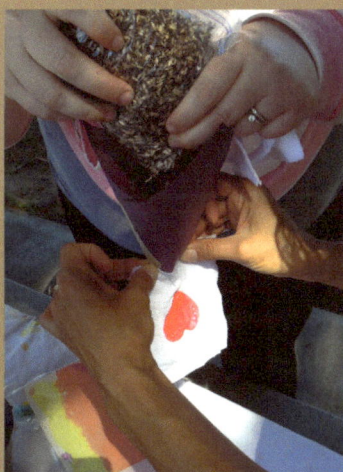

THE TALE OF TOM KITTEN ✻ 42

Make Scented Paint & Decorate Cards

Materials:
- 1/2 cup baking soda
- 4 TBSP white vinegar
- 1 tsp light corn syrup
- 4 TBSP cornstarch
- food coloring
- items to add scent (lemon, orange, lavender, bottled extracts)
- grater, mortar and pestle (optional)
- measuring cups and spoons
- bucket for mixing base, individual cups/jars for mixing in colors/scents
- stir sticks (we used craft sticks)
- whisk
- paper towels, soap and water for cleaning hands
- pre-cut watercolor card paper
- paint brushes

*It is recommended to make paint a day before using it, but that wasn't possible for our schedule, and the experience of pouring and mixing was one of the highlights of the kids' day.

NOTES

Here's our color/scent combo:
orange- grated orange rind
yellow- grated lemon rind
purple- ground lavender
green- mint extract

Steps:
1. Arrange materials in 2 stations: paint-making and fragrance-prepping.
2. Invite kids to choose a station to begin working. They can switch places at some point.
3. Pour baking soda into bucket. Add vinegar, stir. Add corn syrup and starch, and mix well.
4. Pour base mixture into jars, and mix in food coloring.

5. While one group mixes paint, the other group to grates and grinds! There are no hard and fast rules here. Graters can be used for orange and lemon rinds, and a mortar and pestle is great for lavender or other herbs. Extracts are easy to add into paint, whether using actual organic material or not. The amount added to the paint depends on how much fragrance you want, but keep in mind that the more organic matter you add to the paint, the clumpier the paint will become.
6. Encourage kids to touch and smell materials they are working with.
7. Bring out the paper and brushes—it's time to design cards. (Name an adult to hold cards for party.)

Button Trail Search

We know that when Tom Kitten climbed a rockery, or rock wall, the buttons on his clothing were shed right and left. We also know that Mr. Drake Puddle-Duck picked up the various articles of clothing belonging to Tom Kitten that had fallen off as he climbed down the rockery. Instead of returning Tom's clothing, Mr. Puddle-Duck put them on *himself* and set off up the road. So this search is to find that rascal of a duck by following the trail of buttons left behind.

Materials:
- duck (stuffed animal or picture)
- buttons
- painted pails
- doll clothing (optional)

Steps:
1. Assign a parent, or older sibling, to make a trail of buttons that ends at the duck.
2. Hand out pails to the children, and explain the objective: to follow the buttons, collecting them in the pails along the way, and find the rascal who took Tom Kitten's buttons (and clothes, if you are using clothes).
3. Set them loose!

THE TALE OF TOM KITTEN ✻ 44

Tom Kitten

LOCATION:	
DATE/TIME:	
SNACK:	

ACTIVITY 1:	
LEADER:	
NOTES:	

ACTIVITY 2:	
LEADER:	
NOTES:	

ACTIVITY 3:	
LEADER:	
NOTES:	

ACTIVITY 4:	
LEADER:	
NOTES:	

NOTES

Jeremy Fisher

Once upon a time there was a frog called Mr. Jeremy Fisher; he lived in a little damp house amongst the buttercups at the edge of a pond.

~Beatrix Potter

The Tale Of Mr Jeremy Fisher

NOTES
Location & Time:
_____

Fun for the day:
- Circle time
- Snack
- Secure lily pads
- Gather worms and sticks for fishing
- Fish amongst the lily pads
- Plant wild flowers

Circle Time Discussion Suggestions:
* characters in the story, including minnows, water-beetle, Jack Sharp the stickleback, trout, Mr. Alderman Ptolemy Tortoise, Sir Isaac Newton
* favorite parts of story
* define, even bring to show, mackintosh (rain coat) and galoshes (waterproof overshoes/rain boots)
* **invite children to share their notebooks**

Fun Facts About Frogs:
* frogs lay their eggs in water, and the eggs hatch into tadpoles with long tails
* frogs can absorb water through their skin so they don't need to drink
* the eyes and nose of a frog are on top of its head so it can breathe and see when most of its body is under water
* a group of frogs is called an army

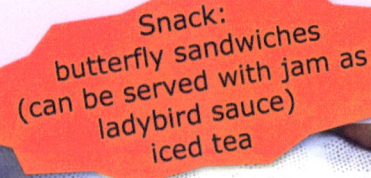

Snack: butterfly sandwiches (can be served with jam as ladybird sauce) iced tea

"I will get some worms and go fishing and catch a dish of minnows for my dinner,' said Mr. Jeremy Fisher."

~ B.P.

Materials (for all fishing-related activities):
- ☐ pre-cut lily pads
- ☐ magnetic worms (*see pre-planning section on pages 74 and 75)
- ☐ white "horsehairs" (pre-cut strips of string)
- ☐ pre-cut paper fish prepped with paper clips
- ☐ painted pails
- ☐ long sticks
- ☐ wood golf tees
- ☐ stones

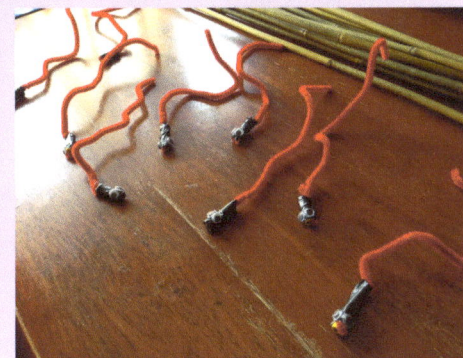

Gather Worms and Sticks for Fishing

Steps:
1. Beforehand, arrange for long sticks, magnetic worms, and string to be scattered around yard, one of each per child. (String may be kept in a central location since it could easily be overlooked if scattered.)
2. Remind children what Mr. Jeremy Fisher used on his fishing day: reed pole (rod); wriggling worms; and fine, long, white horsehair (line). Encourage them to consider what they might find around the yard that would help them catch fish.
3. Supply them each with a painted pail, and send them off to gather their materials.

Secure Lily Pads

Steps:
1. Using the stones, children can pound the golf tees through the pre-cut lily pads to secure a path from one side of the "lake" to the other. (We made a path of lily pads from our circle time blanket to the planting station.)

THE TALE OF MR. JEREMY FISHER

Fishing Amongst the Lily Pads

Now that the children have their fishing poles and worms, and the lily pads are in place, it's time to go fishing!

NOTES

51 ✻ BEATRIX POTTER BOOK CLUB ORGANIZER

Planting Wild Flower Sprouts

The family who volunteered to care for the seeds planted in eggshells during the day of fun with Jemima Puddle-Duck should bring the sprouting flowers with them for this activity. If possible, arrange to plant seeds at a location where the final party will be held so the sprouts can be kept and cared for by that family. Pots will be distributed at the party.

This is a good chance for the children to play in the mud!

Materials:
- ☐ sprouts in eggshells
- ☐ soil
- ☐ painted pots and trays
- ☐ hand trowels or large spoons
- ☐ water

NOTES

Step 1. Fill pots with moist soil, and make an egg-sized hole in the middle.

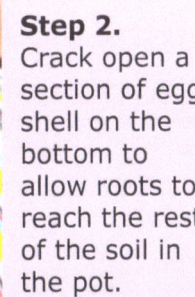

Step 2. Crack open a section of egg shell on the bottom to allow roots to reach the rest of the soil in the pot.

Step 3. Place egg in the hole in the soil, sprouts up, and bring the soil up to the edge of the egg shell.

Step 4. Sprinkle with water, and if you happen to have a small toy frog, leave it in the pot to guard the sprouts. :)

Jeremy Fisher

LOCATION:	
DATE/TIME:	
SNACK:	

ACTIVITY 1:	
LEADER:	
NOTES:	

ACTIVITY 2:	
LEADER:	
NOTES:	

ACTIVITY 3:	
LEADER:	
NOTES:	

ACTIVITY 4:	
LEADER:	
NOTES:	

NOTES

Mrs. Tittlemouse

&

BEATRIX POTTER PARTY

Once upon a time there was a wood-mouse, and her name was Mrs. Tittlemouse. She lived in a bank under a hedge.

~Beatrix Potter

The Tale Of Mrs. Tittlemouse

Fun for the day:
- Circle time (at the table)
- Meal
- Mrs. Tittlemouse puppet show
- Presentations
- Benjamin Bunny treasure hunt
- Decorating envelopes
- Photo op!
- Collecting plants in painted pots, painted pails, and sachets & cards in envelopes

Circle Time Discussion Suggestions:
* characters in the story, including Mother Ladybird, spider, Babbitty Bumble, Mr. Jackson, creepy-crawly bugs "people," Miss Butterfly, five other mice for party
* favorite parts of story
* **invite children to share their notebooks**

Fun Facts About Mice:
* mice in the wild eat grains and fruits
* their tails can grow as long as their bodies
* they have poor eyesight but make up for this with their excellent sense of smell

MENU

Pound Cake
Tea
Cookies, Cupcakes, Macaroons
Chicken Pot Pie (homemade by 11-year-old older brother)
Egg Salad Sandwiches and Cucumber and Cream Cheese Sandwiches in Bunny Shapes
Veggies & Dip

NOTES

First-Class Service

Arrange who will be serving your little bunnies, and if there are available older siblings, invite them to serve the younger as they pour tea, offer sandwiches, and plunk sugar cubes. Many hands make light work!

Fine Dining and a Puppet Show

A lovely tea party can be pulled together with simple plastic play dishes and a couple treats, or with elegant glassware and a feast, depending on what your party pals want to do and what you have available. The main thing to keep in mind is your goal:

A JOYFUL TIME WITH YOUR LITTLE BUNNIES AND THEIR BUNNY FRIENDS!

NOTES

Mrs. Tittlemouse Puppet Show

"Mrs. Tittlemouse was a most terribly tidy particular little mouse, always sweeping and dusting the soft sandy floors." ~ B.P.

Some of the older siblings decided they would like to reenact the story of Mrs. Tittlemouse for the little ones by putting on a puppet show.

First, they met at our local bookstore to go over the story and decide the logistics: who would play which character, what props were needed, etc. They rehearsed it a few times and then each cast member took home a copy to practice until the final production.

On the day of the party, the narrator and characters rehearsed several times after setting the stage (a covered table with props).

Final Production

Rehearsal at Bookstore

61 ✻ BEATRIX POTTER BOOK CLUB ORGANIZER

Presentations

We always culminate a book club with a presentation.

Several weeks before our final party, we encourage the children to select a poem or passage from one of Beatrix Potter's stories to recite for the others.

Parents will help them rehearse at home each day leading up to the party. They can bring props if they would like. They also may just choose to show something from their notebooks while sitting on their parent's lap. Some may choose to opt out altogether, and that's okay!

We want the children to encourage and celebrate their friends' efforts without unnecessary pressure or guilt. Perhaps this time they just cheer everyone on, and the next time they realize it's not so scary and join the fun.

NOTES

Benjamin Bunny's Treasure Hunt

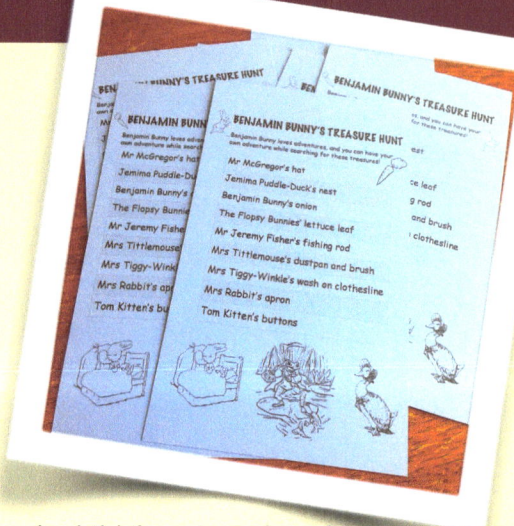

NOTES

Materials:
- ☐ a copy of Treasure Hunt list for each child (see templates)
- ☐ painted pails for collected items
- ☐ Mr. McGregor's hat (straw hat)
- ☐ Jemima Puddle-Duck's nest (Easter/spring nest decor or vines/sticks bound together in circle
- ☐ Benjamin Bunny's onion (large raw onion)
- ☐ the Flopsy Bunnies' lettuce leaf
- ☐ Mr. Jeremy Fisher's fishing rod (one of the rods from previous meeting)
- ☐ Mrs. Tittlemouse's dustpan and brush (dust pan and hand brush)
- ☐ Mrs. Tiggy-Winkle's wash on clothesline (thin rope/yarn, clothing, clothespins
- ☐ Mrs. Rabbit's apron (any apron)
- ☐ Tom Kitten's buttons (either buttons in a jar, or scattered about)

Steps:
1. "Hide" items ahead of time in your designated area for the treasure hunt.
2. Explain to the kids what they are looking for.
3. Distribute pails and lists to each child and send them on their way.

Assign one parent to oversee the envelope-decorating station. Decide on an ideal time for this activity. It worked best for us to keep them out from under our feet as we set the food tables.

Decorating Gift Envelopes

Materials:
- envelopes big enough to hold sachet and gift card
- stencils (optional)
- markers, colored pencils, or crayons

Steps:
1. Place envelopes and art supplies before the children.
2. Make sure their names are on the envelopes.
3. Place each sachet and card in the appropriate envelope.

NOTES

Take Home a Pot

It's time for the kids to receive the rewards of their hard work! Before leaving the party, make sure they take their potted plants and envelopes (with sachets and cards) home.

After our meal had ended, one parent placed the name cards on each pot to make it easier for the kids to find the one belonging to them. And it made for a pretty picture.

*Suggestion: bring large paper bags for each family to transport pot home.

NOTES

Say "Cheese" for Final Pictures

Need I say more? Pictures are a MUST!

Tip: As we wrap up a book club, I enjoy printing collages for the kids using pictures taken throughout the weeks. They love looking through these pictures, and it makes an inexpensive gift that keeps on giving!

THE TALE OF MRS. TITTLEMOUSE ~ PARTY

Mrs. Tittlemouse ~ Party

LOCATION:	
DATE/TIME:	
SNACK:	

ACTIVITY 1:	
LEADER:	
NOTES:	

ACTIVITY 2:	
LEADER:	
NOTES:	

ACTIVITY 3:	
LEADER:	
NOTES:	

ACTIVITY 4:	
LEADER:	
NOTES:	

NOTES:

That's the end of our story...

now it's time to write yours.

But before you begin, here is a behind-the-scenes look at the helping hands and pre-meeting prep.

The older siblings so often mentioned...

A BIG thanks to them! We couldn't have done it without them.

When they weren't scattering Tom Kitten's buttons or hiding the treasure hunt items, they could be found clowning around or playing games together. I only wish I would have taken a picture of all of them together.

Thank you, Maddie, Olivia, William, Jackson, Truman, Preston, Christopher, and Jaden!

Pre-Planning

Some of us on a late-night cutting and sanding spree, but not without lots of laughing and chatting!

Before the fun begins with your little ones, let's get to work with some pre-planning!

We all know the saying, "Many hands make light work." This is especially true for a group gathering involving jumpy, bubbly children. The more you can think through some of the basic elements ahead of time, knowing how to utilize the advantage of teamwork, the smoother things will go. The less jumbly mommy brains and overall confusion, the better! Happy planning!

GET SOME PEP IN YOUR STEP, BY STARTING YOUR PREP . . .

Here's what we'll tackle:

- ☐ collect jars, containers, cans, spoons, trowels, old pillowcases, and sheets
- ☐ sand pots
- ☐ wipe down pails
- ☐ clean eggshells
- ☐ make magnetic "worms"
- ☐ cut felt patterns for bunny ears
- ☐ prepare sachet fabric
- ☐ cut lily pads
- ☐ assemble bunny books (notebooks)
- ☐ cut bookmarks
- ☐ cut greeting cards
- ☐ cut fish shapes
- ☐ label and cut name cards for final tea party
- ☐ print and cut treasure hunt list

1. **Use the note sections and tables provided throughout and at the end of each story section to record the following:**

   - schedule and location
   - snacks—what will be served, and who will provide? Alternating is recommended.
   - designate who will run each activity and provide necessary materials

2. **Tips to consider when establishing expenses:**

   - after deciding on specific activities, determine which materials can be donated by the book club participants and which need to be purchased
   - take advantage of current sales and coupons
   - make the most of the educator discounts at arts and crafts stores and bookstores

Collect:

You are bound to find many of the needed items listed below in your recycling bins, gardening materials, and linen closets. The more you can gather together, the lower the material expense will be.

- empty jars, cans, canisters
- old pillowcases (I also found some at the local dollar store)
- spoons or hand trowels
- smooth stones
- long, sturdy sticks for fishing poles

Pre-Planning Steps ✱ 72

Sand Pots:

You will need terra cotta pots and trays, fine grit sandpaper (I used 220), a damp rag, and newspaper.

1. Over newspaper, gently sand all surfaces of pots and trays. (This can get a little messy!)
2. Wipe down with damp rag.
3. Store pots and trays stacked one on top of the other, lined with a layer of newspaper between each.

Wipe Down Pails:

You will need a damp rag.

1. Remove any price tags.
2. Wipe down pail with damp rag.

Clean Eggshells:

You will need uncooked eggs (one per child, plus a few extra in case of breaking), bowl to collect eggs, individual egg carton cups cut from carton, sharp knife or toothpick, soap, and container with lid.

1. Carefully crack eggs toward the top, approximately 3/4 way up, and pour contents of egg into a bowl.
2. Under running water, rinse egg with soapy water.
3. Gently poke a few holes in bottom of egg with toothpicks, let air-dry, then store in container.

Make Magnetic Worms:

You will need pipe cleaners, magnets, tape, strong glue, and wiggly eyes. *We used hot glue for eyes, magnetic tape (Walmart), and magnets from Geomag (Geomagworld) but other styles work.*

1. Tape the magnet to the pipe cleaner, leaving tip of magnet uncovered. (Magnet will need to be strong enough to attach to paper clips on fish.
2. Attach eyes with glue.

Prepare Bunny Ears:

You will need various colors of felt (unless you choose to make a different style of bunny ears with card stock paper or other materials), popsicle sticks, hot glue, and template in the back of this guide.

1. Cut ears out of felt, in pairs.
2. Hot glue popsicle sticks to half of ear shapes (Only one side of ear needs a stick to give it shape.)

Prepare Sachets:

You will need flour sack towels (we bought ours at Walmart, and 1 pack was more than enough for 10 sachets), pins, and sewing machine (or needle and thread if sewing by hand).

1. Cut desired shapes out of towels, in pairs.
2. Pin pair together, then sew all four sides, leaving opening for lavender to be added with children during the week of Tom Kitten.

   *We only left an inch for opening, which was too small to add lavender easily. I would recommend a 2-inch opening.

   **You can choose to iron fabric before sewing, but we chose to leave it as it came in the package because we liked the textured look.

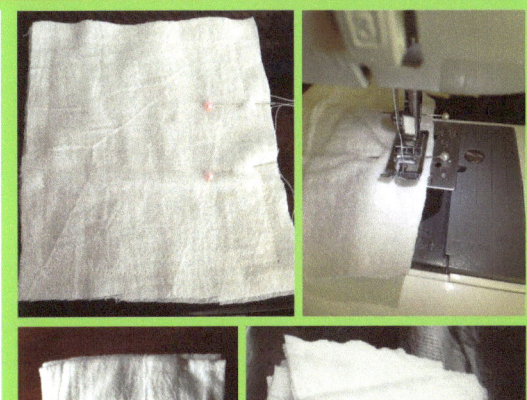
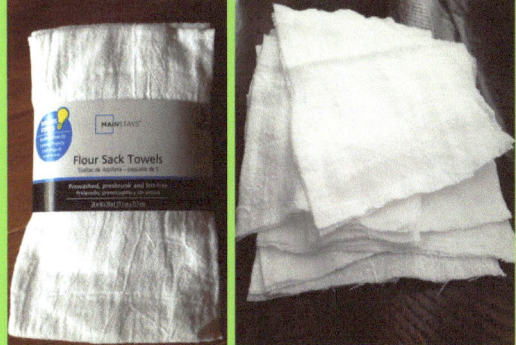

Cut Lily Pads:

You will need scissors, template from back of this guide, and green fabric or other thick green material such as foam sheets.

1. Trace template onto fabric.
2. Cut out lily pad shapes.

   Tip: *If you are making lily pads out of paper, the size I provided in the back of this book will suffice. If, however, you choose to make your lily pads out of fabric and nail them into the grass, you may want to make your lily pads slightly larger. When the fabric is nailed into the grass, some material is pulled down, leaving less material for the kids to step on.*

Bind Notebooks:

You will need card stock paper, standard paper, ribbon, hole punch, and scissors (or paper slicer).

1. Trim 1/2 inch off top of standard sheets, then fold in half, widthwise. (We used 10 sheets per book and trimmed tops so they weren't so big.)
2. Fold card stock in half and staple, or hole punch and bind with ribbon.

Prepare Cards & Bookmarks:

You will need paper, ribbon, pencil and hole punch. *Watercolor paper gives best results with paint.*

1. Mark size of bookmarks and cards, and fold along lines.
2. Slowly tear along lines for rough edges, or cut with scissors.

Fish:

You will need colored paper, scissors, and template.

1. Copy fish outlines onto your colored paper, using template.
2. Cut fish shapes.
3. Allow your child to draw eyes if they would like. (See right photo.)
4. Attach paper clips now, or day of activity.

Create Name Cards:

You will need scissors, template, pen, and paper of your choice. (We used a cream-colored card stock.)

1. Write names of each child on their own card.
2. Cut individual name cards along dotted lines.
3. Fold in half so they will stand up on table at tea party.

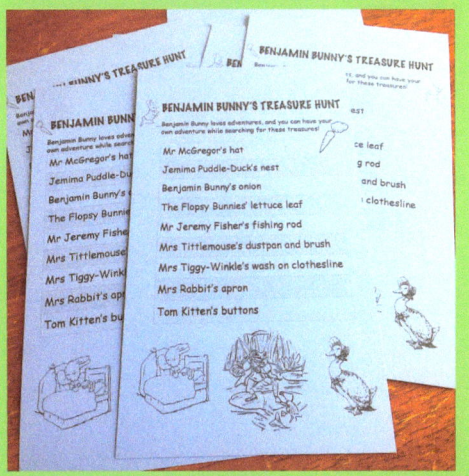

Copy Treasure Hunt Lists:

You will need scissors, template, pen, and paper of your choice. (We used card stock.)

1. Make enough copies to give to each child. (Each template sheet contains two lists.)
2. Cut each sheet in half.

Pre-Planning Steps ✻ 76

Shopping List & Templates

Visit 'Book Clubs' at
WWW.LETSLEARNKIDS.COM
for printing these shopping lists and templates.

SHOPPING LIST

Extra spaces are provided for you to add additional materials.

HOME ITEMS TO REPURPOSE (NON-RETURNABLE)

- [ ] Pillowcases (1 per child) **FB**
- [ ] Newspaper **PR BB**
- [ ] Eggshells for egg planters (1 per child) **JP**
- [ ] Stuffing from an old pillow or two **JP**
- [ ] Paprika and tumeric spices (optional) **JP**
- [ ] Tins, jars, and cans (empty) **FB TK**
- [ ]
- [ ]
- [ ]

ITEMS TO PURCHASE AS I GO (PERISHABLE)

- [ ] Eggs for coloring **JP**
- [ ] Orange for orange zest (scented paint) **TK**
- [ ] Lemon zest (scented paint) **TK**
- [ ] Red cabbage **JP**
- [ ] Brewed coffee **JP**
- [ ] Fresh veggies (lettuce, squash, carrots) **FB**
- [ ]
- [ ]
- [ ]

HOME ITEMS TO REPURPOSE (RETURNABLE)

- [ ] Buttons (the bigger the better) **TK**
- [ ] Towels and rags **PR TW TK**
- [ ] Hole punch for Bunny Book **PR**
- [ ] Wash basin or tub **TW**
- [ ] Wicker laundry basket (optional) **TW FB**
- [ ] Slotted spoon **JP**
- [ ] Spray bottle **JP JF**
- [ ] River rocks or kid's wooden hammer for pounding **PR JF**
- [ ] Digging spoons or hand trowels **BB JP FB JF**
- [ ] Articles of clothing **TW**

NATURE ITEMS TO GATHER

- [ ] Dried lavender for paint and sachets **PR TK**
- [ ] Sticks for fishing rods (1 per child) **JF**
- [ ] Plant vines or sticks **JP**
- [ ]
- [ ]
- [ ]
- [ ]
- [ ]
- [ ]
- [ ]

HANDY-DANDY KEY

PR—Peter Rabbit
BB—Benjamin Bunny
TW—Mrs. Tiggy-Winkle
JP—Jemima Puddle-Duck

FB—Flopsy Bunnies
TK—Tom Kitten
JF—Jeremy Fisher
TM—Mrs. Tittlemouse

SHOPPING LIST

ITEMS TO PURCHASE BEFORE BOOK CLUB (NON-PERISHABLE)

- [ ] Plastic sandwich bags (large and small), for storing items **TW TK**
- [ ] Dish soap **PR BB TW JP TK**
- [ ] Soil for planting **JP JF**
- [ ] Seeds for planting **JP**
- [ ] Heavy paper for Bunny Book cover (card stock, etc.) **PR**
- [ ] Standard paper for Bunny Book filler sheets **PR**
- [ ] Ribbon for Bunny Book binding (thin) **PR**
- [ ] Glue (extra-strength)
- [ ] Decorations for Bunny Book (stickers, stencils, buttons, dried flowers, markers, etc.) **PR**
- [ ] Craft Glue for felt bunny ears **PR**
- [ ] Felt (various colors) **PR**
- [ ] Wooden craft sticks (popsicle sticks) **PR TK**
- [ ] Thread (various colors) **PR**
- [ ] Bells (small, only 1 per set of bunny ears) **PR**
- [ ] Cotton balls (1 bag) **PR**
- [ ] Sewing needles (large are easier for small hands to hold) **PR**
- [ ] Planter pots and drip trays (terra cotta) **BB**
- [ ] Paint (acrylic or patio paint) **PR BB TW**
- [ ] Sand paper (fine grit—around 220) **BB**
- [ ] Stencils (bendable to wrap around pot), or stamps **PR BB TW**
- [ ] Foam brushes and paint brushes **PR BB TW TK**
- [ ] Tape **TK**

- [ ] Clear acrylic sealer (I used spray version; it's unnecessary with patio paint) **PR BB**
- [ ] Clothespins (wooden for authentic look) **TW**
- [ ] Yellow rubber gloves (2 per child) **TW**
- [ ] Safety pins **PR**
- [ ] Pipe cleaners (1 per child) **JF**
- [ ] Yarn or rope for clothesline and finish lines **BB TW FB**
- [ ] Magnets - suitable size and shape to attach to end of pipe cleaner. We used magnets from Geomag (Geomagworld) (1 per child) **JF**
- [ ] Magnetic tape (optional) **JF**
- [ ] Green foam, or heavy fabric **JF**
- [ ] Golf tees (or long nails, stakes) **JF**
- [ ] Sachet fabric (dish towels, flour cloth) **TW TK**
- [ ] Distilled white vinegar **JP**
- [ ] Small pails with handles (1 per child) **PR JP TK JF TM**
- [ ] Watercolor paper **PR TK**
- [ ] Waxed paper **PR**
- [ ] Baking soda **TK**
- [ ] Light corn syrup **TK**
- [ ] Cornstarch **TK**
- [ ] Food coloring **TK**
- [ ] Balloons or light balls (2-5) **TW**
- [ ] Washboard for laundry (optional) **TW**
- [ ] Paperclips (metal) **JF**

SHOPPING LIST

ITEMS TO PURCHASE BEFORE BOOK CLUB (NON-PERISHABLE)

- [ ] Googly-Eyes **JF**
- [ ] String (preferably white) **JF**
- [ ] Envelopes (1 per child, and big enough to hold sachet and card) **TM**

HANDY-DANDY KEY

PR—Peter Rabbit
BB—Benjamin Bunny
TW—Mrs. Tiggy-Winkle
JP—Jemima Puddle-Duck

FB—Flopsy Bunnies
TK—Tom Kitten
JF—Jeremy Fisher
TM—Mrs. Tittlemouse

BENJAMIN BUNNY'S TREASURE HUNT

Benjamin Bunny loves adventures, and you can have your own adventure while searching for these treasures!

- Mr. McGregor's hat
- Jemima Puddle-Duck's nest
- Benjamin Bunny's onion
- The Flopsy Bunnies' lettuce leaf
- Mr. Jeremy Fisher's fishing rod
- Mrs. Tittlemouse's dustpan and brush
- Mrs. Tiggy-Winkle's wash on clothesline
- Mrs. Rabbit's apron
- Tom Kitten's buttons

BENJAMIN BUNNY'S TREASURE HUNT

Benjamin Bunny loves adventures, and you can have your own adventure while searching for these treasures!

- Mr. McGregor's hat
- Jemima Puddle-Duck's nest
- Benjamin Bunny's onion
- The Flopsy Bunnies' lettuce leaf
- Mr. Jeremy Fisher's fishing rod
- Mrs. Tittlemouse's dustpan and brush
- Mrs. Tiggy-Winkle's wash on clothesline
- Mrs. Rabbit's apron
- Tom Kitten's buttons

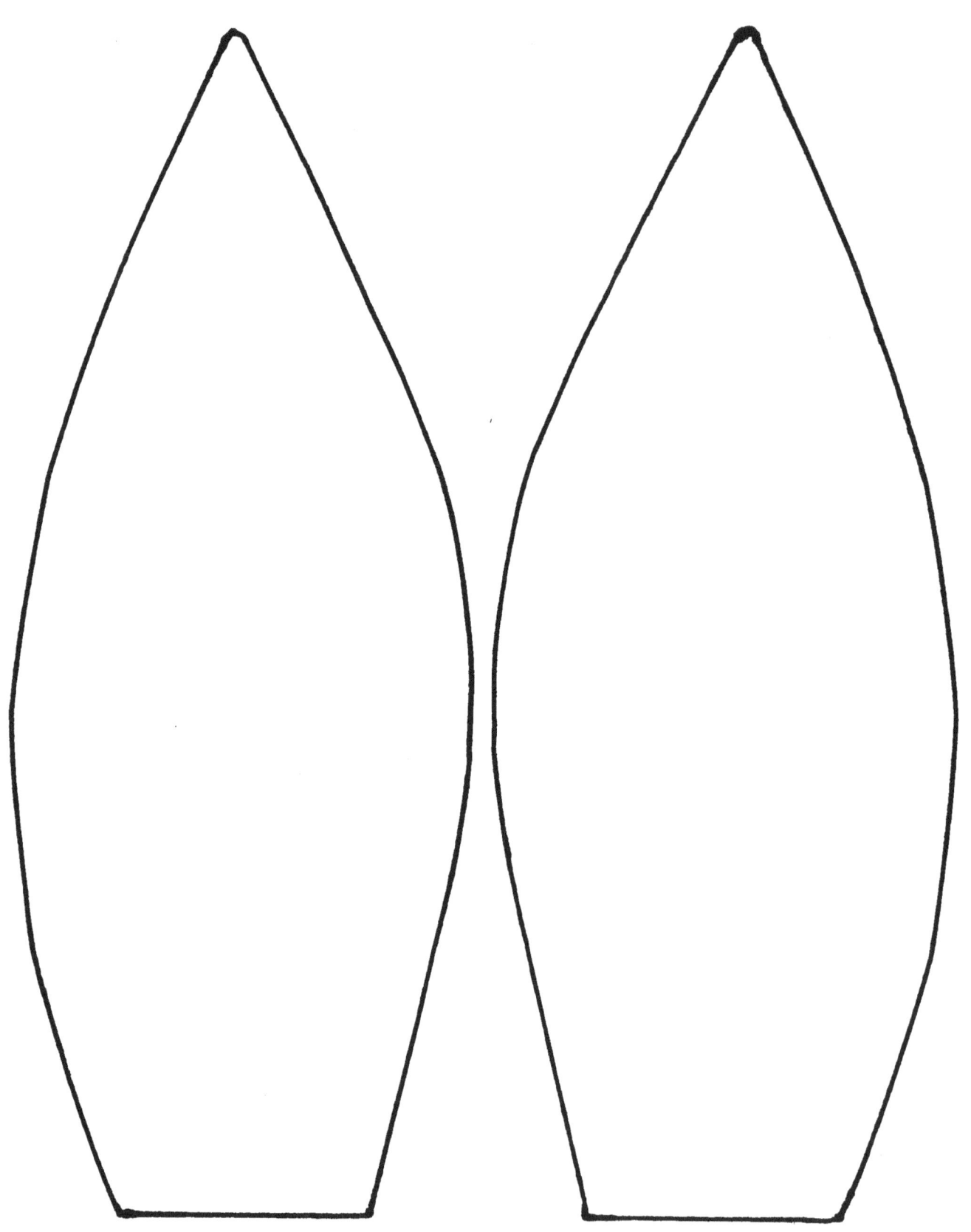

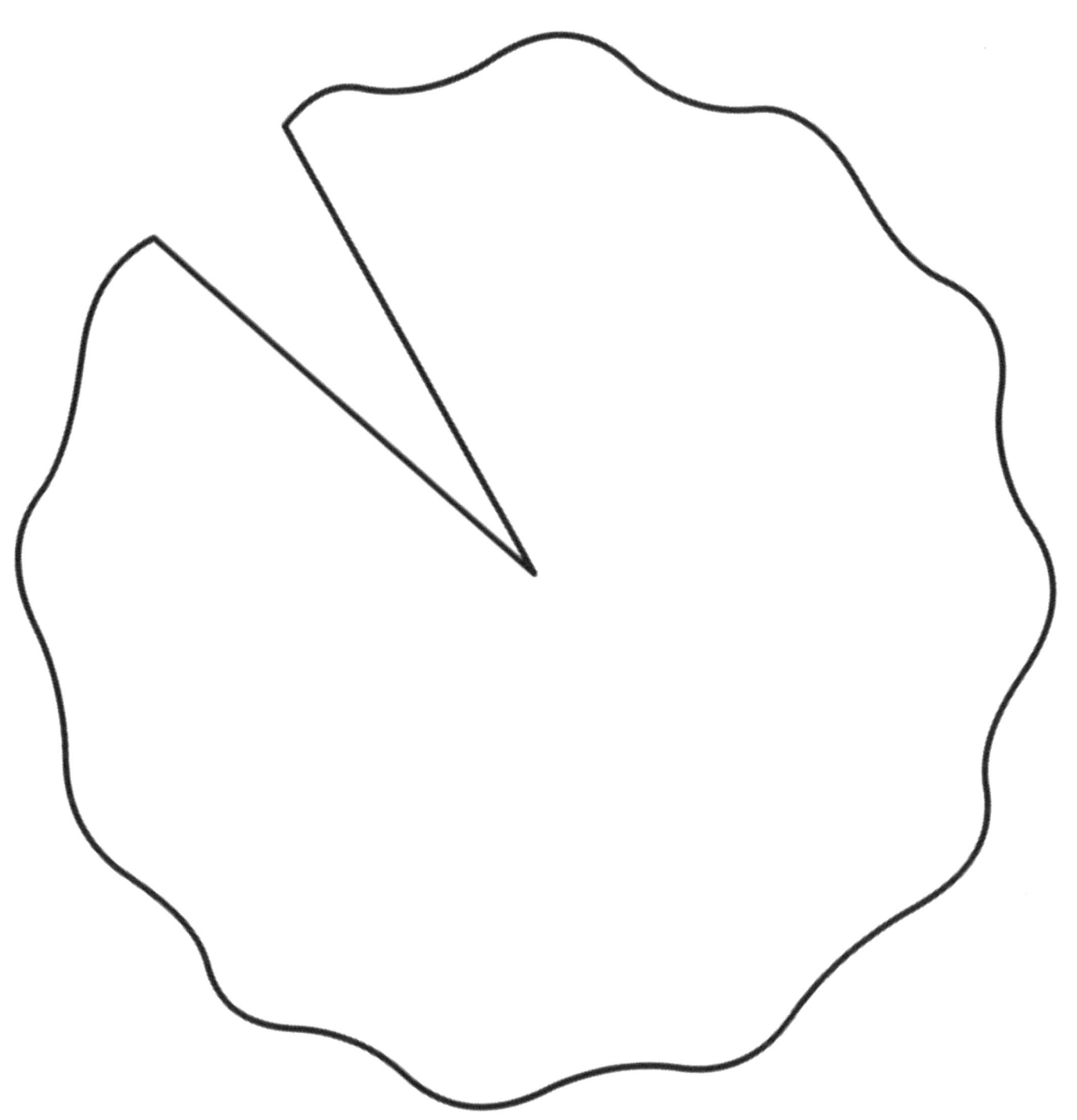

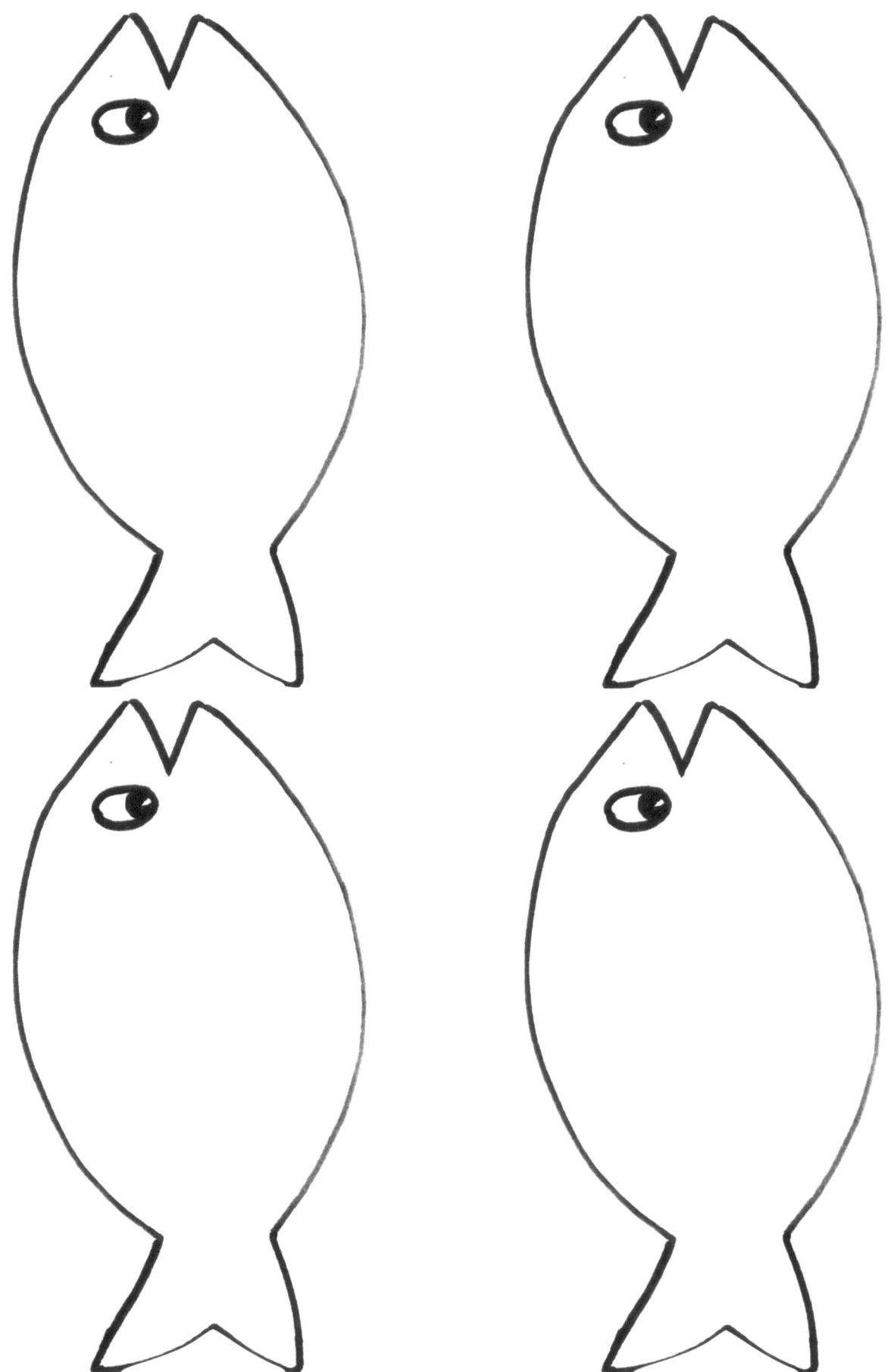

www.ingramcontent.com/pod-product-compliance
Lightning Source LLC
Chambersburg PA
CBHW041124300426
44113CB00002B/48